Baby Snow Animals

Jane Katirgis

T0002556

Bailey Books
an imprint of
Enslow Publishers, Inc.
40 Industrial Road
Box 398
Berkeley Heights, NJ 07922
USA
http://www.enslow.com

Bailey Books, an imprint of Enslow Publishers, Inc.

Copyright © 2011 by Enslow Publishers, Inc.

Library of Congress Cataloging-in-Publication Data

Katirgis, Jane.

Baby snow animals / Jane Katirgis.

    p. cm. — (All about baby animals)

Includes bibliographical references and index.

Summary: "Introduces pre-readers to simple concepts about snow animals using short sentences and repetition of words"—Provided by publisher.

ISBN 978-0-7660-3797-7

1. Tundra animals—Infancy—Polar regions—Juvenile literature. I. Title.

QL104.K38 2011

591.75'86—dc22   2010011888

Paperback ISBN: 978-1-59845-160-3

Printed in the United States of America

052015 Bang Printing, Brainerd, MN

10 9 8 7 6 5 4 3 2

Photo Credits: age fotostock/photolibrary, p. 6–7; © David Pike/naturepl.com, pp. 3 (nap), 4–5; © iStockphoto.com: Andy Gehrig, p. 22, © Keith Szafranski, pp. 1, 3 (slide), 8–9, © Len Tillim, p. 14, Andrey Artykov, p. 18; Shutterstock.com, pp. 3 (snow), 10–11, 12, 16; © Katherine Feng/Minden Pictures, p. 20.

Cover Photo: © iStockphoto.com/Keith Szafranski.

Note to Parents and Teachers

Help pre-readers get a jumpstart on reading. These lively stories introduce simple concepts with repetition of words and short simple sentences. Photos and illustrations fill the pages with color and effectively enhance the text. Free Educator Guides are available for this series at www.enslow.com. Search for the *All About Baby Animals* series name.

Contents

Words to Know

nap   slide   snow

In the snow,
a baby naps.

**In the snow,
a baby jumps.**

In the snow,
a baby slides.

9

In the snow, a baby rests.

In the snow,
a baby hugs.

In the snow, a
baby stays safe.

In the snow,
a baby sits.

In the snow,
a baby walks.

In the snow,
a baby plays.

**In the snow,
a baby grows up.**

Read More

Lee, Jeanie. *Baby Snow Friends.* New York: Little Simon/Simon & Schuster, 2006.

Spinelli, Eileen. *Polar Bear, Arctic Hare: Poems of the Frozen North.* Honesdale, Pa.: Wordsong, 2007.

Web Sites

Enchanted Learning. *Arctic Animals.*
<http://www.enchantedlearning.com>
Click on "Biomes." Then click on "Arctic" or "Antarctic."

National Geographic. *Animals.*
<http://animals.nationalgeographic.com>
Click on "Animal Photos."

Index

Guided Reading Level: B
Guided Reading Leveling System is based on the guidelines recommended by Fountas and Pinnell.

Word Count: 62